This Book Belongs To ----------------

NAME

PHONE

EMAIL

Made in the USA
Monee, IL
27 November 2021

83229919R00056